Reflections
on Life, Living, and Spirituality

REFLECTIONS
on Life, Living, and Spirituality

HENRY C. HAEFNER

LEONINE PUBLISHERS
PHOENIX, AZ

Copyright © 2017 Henry C. Haefner

All rights reserved. No part of this book may be reproduced or transmitted in any form or by any means, electronic or mechanical, including photocopying, recording, or by any information storage or retrieval system now existing or to be invented, without written permission from the respective copyright holder(s), except for the inclusion of brief quotations in a review.

The Scripture citations used in this work are taken from *The Catholic Bible: New American Bible*, Personal Study Edition, copyright © 1995, by Oxford University Press, Inc.

Published by Leonine Publishers LLC
Phoenix, Arizona
USA

ISBN-13: 978-1-942190-32-5
Library of Congress Control Number: 2017941964

Printed in the United States of America
10 9 8 7 6 5 4 3 2 1

Visit us online at www.leoninepublishers.com
For more information: info@leoninepublishers.com

To the glory of the Holy Spirit.

Contents

Humility: L-a-u-g-h-t-e-r Is the Best Medicine ... 1
Scriptures ... 7
Hebrews 3:13 ... 13
Mantras ... 17
Friendship ... 23
Tithing ... 29
If I Felt Any Better, I Would Be in Heaven ... 35
The Best Goodbye ... 39
Children Are Special ... 43
Getting Older ... 47
Throw Away Society ... 51
Pray Always, and If Necessary, Use Words ... 55
Tempus Fugit; Memento Mori ... 61
Peer Pressure ... 65
Tunnel Vision ... 69
Too Much, Too Much, Too Much ... 73
Hello Young Man; Hello Young Lady ... 77
Poverty ... 81
Marriage Between Persons of the Same Gender ... 85
Singing in Church ... 91
Beware—Devils Do Exist ... 95
Our Enemy Is the Devil ... 99
Holiness ... 101
Spreading the Good News ... 107
Illiterate Nation ... 111
Nation Without a Place for Mary ... 115

Humility: L-A-U-G-H-T-E-R Is the Best Medicine

Years ago, the expression "Laughter is the Best Medicine" encouraged people to not take themselves or life too seriously. If we laughed at troubles or events, it eased the stress in our lives. If a person could laugh at himself or his own silly actions, it was even better. The little magazine "Readers Digest" printed a popular section in each issue with jokes and short anecdotes intended to help readers laugh and see humor in life.

But there is perhaps another approach that can be used to relieve stress in a person's life, one that will take away far more stress than even humor or laughter. Let us modify the phrase to: Humility is the Best Medicine.

What is humility? The dictionary says that humility is the quality or state of being humble. But what does it mean to be humble? This word derives from the French *humus* which means *earth* and the Latin *humilis,* which means *low*. To be *humble* is to be low: low in status, low in society and in one's own estimation.

It is often described in negative terms such as "not proud, not haughty, not arrogant nor assertive." It can mean to give up one's own power or to be submissive.

We see examples of humility everywhere in everyday life. Children obey their parents and teachers. The children may not always like what they are asked to do, but in a spirit of obedience they humbly submit and do it, even if they might complain a bit.

Another example comes from the book *A Tale of Two Cities* when the "look alike" person takes the place of the condemned man so that the condemned man can flee to his beloved, get married, and have a family. This exquisite act of charity also showed great humility.

A Catholic priest performed a similar act of charity and humility during World War II. Some of the town's Nazi prisoners had escaped, so the Nazis wanted to punish the town as an example for others. They selected ten citizens to be taken away and executed. But a local priest saw a high degree of stress and anxiety in one of the selected victims, and heard the impassioned pleas of this man. The priest asked permission to take the man's place. The Nazis granted his request, took the priest and nine others to a cave, and executed them by bullets to the back of the head.

From these heroic acts of valiant charity one begins to understand that charity is an integral element of humility. Willingly reducing oneself to the level of *humus*, the earth, is an important step in one's journey to develop the virtue of charity. Sometimes it is very hard to avoid arrogance, or excessive assertiveness when asked to do some things, or to not be proud when we accomplish something well. Without charity as an essential foundation stone, a person cannot achieve the virtue of humility.

Can the virtue of humility be attained readily—overnight? Absolutely not. For, as the philosopher Aristotle indicated, virtues take a long time, if not a lifetime, of repetitive conduct to develop. Just read Aristotle's description of such virtues in his book on the Nicomachean Ethics.

Virtues are developed by repeated conduct over an entire lifetime. If the virtuous acts are not performed over and over again then the virtue can slip away and be eventually lost.

A virtuously humble person will not be stressed in their life. He or she will act with charity, and this does much to soothe the soul and calm the person who is humble.

A virtue consists of repeated acts. The virtue of being truthful is the repeated conduct of telling the truth and of not lying. The virtue of generosity can be shown by almsgiving, repeatedly giving alms to those in great need of money or of help in living. The humble person sees himself as being lowly and not haughty, not envious, not proud, not arrogant. A truly humble person sees himself as being no higher than the lowest of the low person in society. And the great example of such a person was Mother Teresa of Calcutta. She founded an order of nuns whose mission in life is to help and serve the lowest people in any society.

Her nuns are forbidden by their Rule to help and assist any but the lowest of the lows. She recognized that many people are willing to help those in some need but not those in desperate need. The lowest are often ignored and loathed. When leprosy was rampant, for example, such people were required to stay apart from the healthy community. They were required to shout out that they were "unclean" to warn the healthy people to stay away.

Once Mother Teresa saw a very elderly woman being placed in a garbage can. The woman wasn't far from death. Her family placed her there because they could no longer afford to keep her since they themselves lived in dire poverty. The elderly woman understood and made no complaints. But Mother Teresa picked up the dying woman, took her to the shelter that she had established, washed and cleaned the dying woman, fed her, and provided a place for her to die with dignity.

A truly humble person will live in peace and calm. Such persons do not look down on others, nor are they envious or greedy. They are respectful of others and are generally willing to assist when needed.

Scriptures

Most of us ignore the Scriptures. We do not even read the Scriptures, let alone study them, or pray them. If asked, most people would admit that they know very little of the Bible stories. But Saint Jerome, who translated the Scriptures into Latin, put it this way: If you don't know the Gospels, you don't know Jesus, and, if you don't know the Scriptures, you don't know God. The Scriptures were, at that time, in three separate languages, which made it difficult for people to get a unified sense of them. Saint Jerome translated them into Latin, which was then the "official" language being used.

His words are full of truth. Yet many would say they know God and they are "friends" of God. But are they truly close to the Lord? Only He can answer that question. But I wonder if they are anchored in Him. Is their knowledge mainly on the surface? Is it extensive or very limited in scope and breadth? Is it just a smattering gleaned from rusty memory from Scripture readings at church or synagogue services?

Most people establish and foster relationships with their spouse, children, friends, business partners, and working associates. They live with, associate with, plan with, spend time with, and share presence with others. Do they not realize that their very existence and lives continue because of the compassion and love of the Lord? All of this is a gift from God. It is unearned, and unmerited. It is simply a gift because of the generous and unconditional love of God.

We spend some or even much of our lives developing and strengthening our relationships with other people, but we do very little or even nothing to develop or strengthen our relationship with the Lord. We continue our relations with our Creator on a surface level. We might know, as Christians, the names of the Father, Son (Jesus), and Holy Spirit, but not much more than that.

My law partner Chuck was a practicing Jew. He knew his Scriptures very well and if others professed a faith, Chuck expected that they should also know and "own" their faith. They should know their faith well.

Sometimes Chuck would test people to see how much they knew about their faith. One evening, my wife Bernadette and I invited Chuck and his wife, Edith, over to our house for supper. Naturally our two young school-aged children, Tony and Colleen, were there also. At one point

Chuck brought up the topic of religion, especially as known through Scripture stories. He asked the kids to tell him the story of Daniel in the lion's den. They proceeded together to tell him the story. I held my breath, hoping they would succeed—and they did! Chuck looked pleased. Two Christian children knew a story from Judaic Scripture (the Old Testament). They knew it well and it was picked at random. That pleased Chuck. But many others failed to pass Chuck's test, as he related such failures to me.

This points to a huge defect in American society. We who profess to be of a faith belief, in reality, know very little at all. Basically, we live on the surface of our faith. We do not take the time, nor make the effort, to "own" our faith. We do not make it "ours." We do not possess it.

After I graduated from high school, I entered the Air Force with a group of my classmates. After basic training I was assigned to an air base in upper-state New York. I was an enlisted man in a bomber squadron of fifty bomber planes, and all of its personnel were transferred to England for five months of training in the European Theater, just in case war began between Communist Russia and the United States. Such were the conditions of what was known as the "Cold War."

As an enlisted person I often did not have any work duties in the evening. Most young enlisted men wanted to go into the nearby village to the tavern for fun and drinking. But at that stage of life I realized that I knew next to nothing of the Scripture stories, whether it was of the Jewish or Christian Scriptures—the Old Testament or the New Testament. So I made a deal with myself. Four nights a week, after work and supper, I stayed in the barracks and read Scripture, from the first page of the Bible to the last. I read for two to three and a half hours each night. That is not the best way to learn the Scriptures, but that is what I did, and I got a fair understanding of the Scripture stories, thank goodness.

In college, I more deeply studied many of the Gospels and parts of the Old Testament. Since then I have done self-studies and I have led Bible study groups for many years.

Am I bragging about what I have done? No. I'm asking: Why aren't many others doing the same? Why aren't others owning their faith?

Not far in the past, scholars ranked the various fields of study in a hierarchical system. Theology was ranked number one and philosophy came in second. Why? Because fields of study were ranked in accord with what was most critical to know for human living. Theology was first and then philosophy.

Society may not now acknowledge theology as the most relevant study, but individually we ought to give it the first position in our lives.

Read and know the Bible!

Own the Scripture stories!

Own your faith!

Share your faith with others!

Know your Catholic Faith, and discuss it with your friends and family members. By doing this you deepen your ownership of your faith and, at the same time, you help others do the same.

Don't be afraid to voice your love and knowledge of the Lord. God knows and loves you and each and every one of us. So, be "Holy Spirit Bold" and deepen your faith.

Hebrews 3:13

In the Epistle of Saint Paul to the Hebrews, chapter three, verse 13, he writes, "But exhort one another every day, whilst it is called today, that none of you be hardened through the deceitfulness of sin."

This Bible verse seems to be saying that we should encourage ourselves and others to do what God wants us to do and to not sin nor do anything evil. It is easy to ignore the teachings of God and to stray from the path of righteousness. So we need to encourage ourselves, and others, to live a life of holiness. This means to live as the Lord has instructed us to live, growing closer to Him. And to not do otherwise.

But I like to stretch this admonition a bit further. I like to encourage others to keep at whatever they have chosen to do and to not let go of their dreams, hopes, and goals.

When our son Tony was in grade school he played basketball. He wasn't the best and the coach did not allow him to play very much, since the coach wanted a winning team. Only the best players got to play. Tony got to play very little, and only when a sub was needed to give another player a short rest.

When Tony reached high school, he did not qualify for the team. He was very disappointed. I sat down with him and asked him to not give up if he enjoyed playing. I told him that many others would not be on a school team but would still like to play. I encouraged him to look around for them and to ask if they would be willing to play on a "pick-up" team. It worked. He had great fun in doing it. He also made new friendships which lasted a long time.

Eventually he and others learned of a neighborhood sport system where neighborhood teams could come and compete in basketball competitions. So Tony and some of his basketball friends formed a team and competed in that organized sport system. Once a week, in the evenings during the school year, they played in a gym at a Boys Club in the city.

I came to every game as a one-person cheering section, and all of the team members appreciated the encouragement.

Tony attended Xavier University in Cincinnati, Ohio. I went to this same Jesuit University. He kept playing "pick-up" basketball and he loved doing it. He never acquired abilities as a scorer but he improved as a defense person. Many wanted him on their team for that, in addition to the fact that he was simply a nice guy.

Without that encouragement in grade school I am not sure that he would have continued his efforts to play a sport that he loved. He never attained to be a professional player. Very few do. But he did love to play. It was healthy to play. He learned and improved in a team sport which he loved. He made many friends and he enjoyed the playing and the friendships.

No matter what a person does, they need encouragement. We need to give it freely and often—even daily. As Saint Paul says, encourage each other daily while it is still today.

But it is easy for me to talk about encouraging my own son. What about encouraging non-family persons, whether they are young or older or even professionals? They are just as deserving of encouragement. It can be a bit intimidating to talk with non-family persons, but we improve by practicing. We ought to be gentle and mild, not just when starting out, but always. And we must always be compassionate in our approach.

As I said, this is easy when I speak of my own son but how can I help others? When I see others doing a good job, I praise them. They respond with a smile and a "thank you." For instance, while going to my grandson's soccer game one day, I passed a teenager. He was exercising by jumping rope and he was doing it very well. I told him. He smiled and said "thank you." Obviously he appreciated the compliment. People, young or older, appreciate compliments. They enjoy recognition of something well done.

When I see people with much devotion for the Lord, I tell them that they are very holy for living with God in their hearts. They deny this, as Americans usually do, but I persist.

I teach religion to a class of fourth-grade children once a week. I am a retired lawyer. Another teacher is a practicing lawyer. On one occasion I praised him for being so generous and compassionate, and for showing so much love for the Lord and for the children he teaches. He just stood there and listened intently. He seemed shocked to hear praise being sent his way. But when I finished he also said "thank you."

I use this approach very much: praise and encouragement. I keep it short and not prolonged. People demonstrate a hunger for this true and simple encouragement.

There is an inherent need in everyone for encouragement and praise. This is not praise for its own sake but praise to affirm the person so that they are encouraged to continue to do well and to improve their skills.

Encourage each other daily while it is still today.

Mantras

A mantra is adopted as a guide for living. The dictionary suggests that it is "counsel" for a person. It can also mean a "formula" as to how to live. I've heard that bishops, of a certain Christian faith, must adopt a mantra to help guide them in their work as a bishop.

During my life I have adopted two mantras and recently a third.

The first one was at the age of eighteen. I had just graduated from high school, in June of 1955. After my Air Force Basic Training, I went to my first permanent base in Plattsburgh, New York, thirty miles south of the Canadian border. In winter, the temperature was extremely cold—with *plenty* of snow.

With little or no money, I read a lot, especially in the base library. I also spent a good amount of time in church for prayer and various liturgies.

The air base was in the northeastern portion of the state, on the northwest side of Lake Champlain. Winter night temperatures averaged between minus ten and minus twenty-five degrees. One night, it reached minus thirty-nine. (These were actual temperatures and not "wind chill" numbers.) The snowfalls seemed endless. How did we survive? One just learns to deal with it.

One evening in late December, I was in the library. I picked a short book on the lives of the saints. I do not recall which particular person I was reading about but there was a saying of his that struck me strongly. He had had to deal with many difficulties in his life and he adopted the motto: *Luctor et emergo.*

Translated from the Latin, it says: "Struggle and come through." When one is challenged with difficult tasks, one should not be afraid of the struggle, for by doing so and working through the difficult tasks, one can succeed and can emerge a better person.

I wrote down this statement, folded the paper, and put it in my wallet. It has been in my wallet even to this time, more than fifty years later. It has also been in my heart since then and has guided my life always, throughout many difficulties.

My high-school grades were not outstanding and so, in the military, I took a few evening high-school classes. I began to feel that I could have done better in school if only I had pushed myself or had been urged to by my parents. I did well in these courses, mainly because I now wanted to try to succeed. I began to take lower-level college evening courses. I also did well in those, and continued on with evening studies. While at this air base I learned of the headquarters at Offutt Air Force Base near Omaha, Nebraska. I heard that one worked a regular forty-hour work week there, and that an excellent college-level evening program was available. I applied and won the appointment to a position at Offutt. I greatly made use of the opportunity and took many evening courses there. When I left the military after nearly five years of service to my country, I had accumulated about two years of college credits.

After that, I had to work hard to pay my own way through the remainder of college and then through law school, sometimes going full time to school and working full time also. (There were even some nights when I lived on the streets.)

Luctor et emergo.

Time passed. I adopted a system of praying known as the Liturgy of the Hours. This type of prayer is based on Psalms taken from the Bible. I mainly say morning prayers and evening prayers.

For morning prayer, we start with Psalm 95. This opening prayer is called the Invitatory. Before praying this Psalm, I read Hebrews 3:13, as mentioned before. I adopted this as a motto as well. I might not remember to use it at all opportunities but I try to do so. One time, I saw a parishioner in church cleaning the windows in the narthex. I stopped and began praising her for all of the service she does for the Church. I told her how awesome she is, how she allows the Lord to live in her heart and to shine through her to all she meets. At that point she sat down on a chair and cried. I had no way of knowing that, shortly before my comments, she had been let go as an aide in the preschool program and told by her supervisor that she was incompetent. She related this to my wife and said how much she appreciated my comments. It was as if the Holy Spirit had led me to this person who was in great need of encouragement.

Watch as you progress through each day. You come in contact with many people. Count how many times you see people praising or encouraging others. Most religions or faith systems indicate that all people are brothers and sisters of ours, and that we are all created by God and are created in the image and likeness of God, per the book of Genesis, but how few act that way. Employ the practice of encouraging others while it is still today.

Recently I adopted a third mantra. It is from the Latin which says: *Tempus fugit, memento mori*. It means: "Time flies, remember death." At my age this mantra has a special relevancy. One's life moves by more quickly than we realize. While we are enjoying life and its activities, and while we are doing things which show that we love and serve the Lord as well as loving and serving our neighbors, we may not have prioritized what we wish to absolutely accomplish in the years we have remaining. We might not be attending to what God wishes us to accomplish. When we light the candle of our life, we know not how long the flame will continue to burn and give light.

So remember: *Luctor et emergo; Tempus fugit, memento mori.* Encourage each other while it is still today.

Friendship

Naturally, we are not meant to be alone. Only a few individuals can sustain such isolation for a highly valued purpose. For most, that purpose is to give honor and glory to God. Some others might sustain isolation due to a poor self-image or a deep depression; may God bless them.

The rest of mankind highly values friendship, and considers it necessary for living. If one does not live in isolation, then one must live in friendship. It is natural and it is helpful. Without friendship people would not want to live. Even if one had everything else in the world, such a person would not want to continue living. Friendship is a main element for humans to be humans. We can say that love is the reason to live. But another name for love is friendship. These words refer to the same thing.

Regardless of the level of friendship, friendships requires two or more people to share time, communications and presence in order to be friends. Love, i.e., friendship, is the force that brings people together and keeps them united. This constitutes a community of persons. This community exists, at least implicitly, by agreement between those persons in the friendship. And such is an agreement or a compact.

Friendships are of various levels of involvement and intensities. The lowest level is what I might call the "passing" friendship. At times, one might pass another while walking. Each might acknowledge the other and perhaps smile at the other while saying "hello" and continue on their way. Two or more might be sitting near each other and begin a short and cordial conversation with each other, such as might occur on public transportation. This is a friendship of being cordial and sharing time and presence together even if it lasts but a short time.

The next level is the "useful" friendship. For example, let us say that my car has two worn-out tires and that it is getting unsafe to continue to drive on them. So I take the car to my mechanic who puts on two new tires in place of the worn ones. I then get a bill (a high one) and I write a check to pay for the tires and for the service. Hence, during this transaction the mechanic and I are friends of usefulness. We might continue in this friendship relationship. We might just continue to respect each other and be very cordial to each other. This is a low level of friendship.

But let me relate how a relation of usefulness grew into a full-blown friendship. As a practicing lawyer I had a general practice of law. I tried to not specialize even though I was a part-time public defender. I did half of my practice in criminal defense law. I also gave legal advice to a credit union. Over time, I got to know the credit union manager (Ray) and his wife (Betty), who was a clerical employee with the credit union. A personal friendship developed between them and myself and my wife Bernadette. This friendship grew and sustained itself until the deaths of Ray and Betty.

After the "useful," is a friendship of "pleasantness." As with all friendships, such requires the presence of each and wanting to spend time together in some pleasant activity, whether it be talking, walking, or some activity liked and desired by those concerned. For example, some college men might like to have a "pick-up" basketball game. They are not a university ball team, but simply guys who want to be active and play basketball, and are glad that there are enough other guys who also like to play.

A friend seeks to keep his friend from committing error. Friends develop care, compassion, and concern for each other. Friends seek to help with the needs of the other. Hence friendship is like a glue that assists in holding friends together.

But let us broaden this thought just a bit. Friendship also helps to hold families together since friendship is an anchor in families. (Remember that friendship is also known as a type of love.) But let us push this idea one step further; friendship helps give cohesion to cities, states, and nations.

How long can friendships last? They can last as long as the other person is a worthy person. That is to say, the friend needs to be a good person. It can last for a long, long time. Just look at some marriages! This is so because the friend is looked upon as another "self." We consider ourselves good people, and we see the friend also as a good person.

This relationship enhances us, for only the loveable are loved. And as we said, friendship is a form of love. This friendship is between people who are good and alike in virtue, and we are spurred on to grow in our virtues.

But we must keep in mind that strong, firm friendships do not mature quickly. Look at marriages. They mature and strengthen over years. Friendships require trust and such does not develop very quickly. Friendship and trust require duration. Why? Because friends need to be familiar with each other, and this develops only with many and various actions over time.

A key element in friendship is the state of character of the friends. The best state of character is the "good." That is, the goodness of each. Each needs to develop virtue. The strongest friendships exist when the friends are good and also virtuous. That is to say, when each is desired and loveable. Such friendship then forms into a type of community.

Each person loves him or her self. We recognize ourselves as worthy and good. The more virtuous and noble we become the more we love ourselves. And, as was said, we perceive a friend as another self. As such we then also love our friend(s). This is especially so when they are as good as we are, or better.

When people come together and continue to adhere and stay together, there is then a community. A community is a group of people who unite for some mutual benefit. Even if it is unspoken, such continual adhesion constitutes an implied agreement.

Tithing

To tithe means to pay or to give a tenth part of your income or possessions, for the support of the Church. Another meaning is that a tithe is a tenth part of something being paid as a voluntary contribution or as a tax, especially for the support of a religious establishment.[1]

Scripture shows that even at the beginning of Judaism, the king of Salem, namely Melchizedek, who was a priest of the God Most High, blessed Abram, after which Abram gave him a tenth of everything.[2] (Abram was later renamed Abraham.)

Such was an established process and tradition of giving a tithe to priests.[3] It was as a type of payment to them for their services.

This is reflected in the book of Numbers, (18:24), when the Levites and priests, were assigned as their heritage the tithes which the Israelites gave as a contribution to the Lord.

---

[1] *Merriam-Webster Dictionary* (Springfield, MA: Merriam-Webster, Inc., 1987).
[2] Genesis 14:18-21
[3] Deuteronomy 26:12

But let us move much further on in Scripture and look in the Gospel of Luke (18:12), where we see the pompous Pharisee, bragging that he was so much better than the tax collector because he fasted twice a week and paid tithes on his entire income.

So we see that throughout our Scriptures, tithing is a firm and well established practice. Throughout the centuries, tithing has been an embedded way of giving back to the Lord, in appreciation for the generous gifts from the Lord.

In Hebrews 7:5 we again note that the descendants of Levi, who receive the office of priesthood, have a commandment according to the law. It is to exact tithes from the people—from their brothers and sisters in the Lord.

Tithing is also an obligation. Tithing is *not* a free-will offering. It is not a personal decision to give or not to give. The only possible reason to not tithe is if the money is needed for the basic necessities of life, for oneself or one's family. No one should endanger their health or life by giving to the Church or to charities and thus deprive one's self, or the family, of the basic necessities of existence.

Free-will offerings can be given over and above the giving of tithes. We see this in Deuteronomy 12:6 when it is mentioned that the people were told to bring their holocausts and sacrifices, offerings and tithes, and their personal contributions, their votives and their free-will offerings to the priests and Temple. Hence, the amounts a person elects to give, on their own, are free-will offerings. Tithing is required by the law of the Lord.

For these tithes were seen as belonging to the Lord and not to the people, as shown in Leviticus 27:30-31, and as such, are sacred to the Lord our God.

We even see that the tithes were not just for the use of the priests, but also for the common good: for the benefit of the alien, the orphan, and the widow so that they may have their fill in their own community. In other words, the tithes were to help those who were in need, whether a priest or not, whether an Israelite or not. Was this the first form of a Social Security system where the poor and the disabled and the widows and orphans and even the "aliens" would not starve?

The priests, in fulfilling their function, would not have sufficient time or energy to earn a separate living for themselves or their families. Therefore God established tithing to meet the needs of those who would be lacking otherwise. Again, the tithes were referred to as God's sacred portion and were to be given in light of the Lord's commandment.

So why have the churches and temples and synagogues drifted away from such an important element of our Catholic, Christian, and Jewish faiths? Why have we ignored this important means to develop the spirituality of our souls by giving of our wealth and caring for others?

Our giving to the Church is an important means for developing a close relationship with the Lord. For one thing, tithing is a law which the Lord established. This law is at the heart of our faith because obedience to it sustains our priests and assists the common good. We desire the eternal salvation of all people, as well as their physical well-being. While we are on the path to salvation, in accord with the law of the Lord, we are to provide for those in need, physically and spiritually. Such is an important and essential element of the "common good." The rich and the poor have a common bond: the Lord is the creator of all. As such we are all brothers and sisters in the Lord. Ought we not to be looking after one another?

Millions of our brothers and sisters starve to death each year, as well as being homeless, or suffering from illnesses or injustices.

If we have sufficient financial means, why do we ignore such needs and close our hearts to such massive sufferings? Why don't we live our faith by caring for the common good? Why do we focus on self-centered visions? Why do we ignore this law of God?

All the faithful—men, women, young, old, laity, priests, vowed, sisters, deacons, brothers, bishops—should seek to re-establish this required and compassionate law of the Lord. This law flows directly from God who is the Creator of all humankind, and from the Sacred Heart of Jesus.

But wait, you say! "I do give to the poor," you say. Does this then suffice, you ask?

Absolutely not. Tithing is not the same as a free-will offering. "But," you say, "I do give to the poor and the homeless and to various charities. Doesn't this suffice?" No, it does not. This is called "almsgiving," which is indeed good and worthy, but vastly separate and different from tithing. We see in Acts 3:2 that the man who was crippled from birth was carried each day to gate, which was called "Beautiful," so that he could beg for alms. People who gave money to him were not tithing; they were giving alms.

In Tobias 4:6-11, we are told to share from our possessions by almsgiving, even if we have little. It states here what rewards the Lord gives to those that share their possessions. In Tobias 4:17 we are told to share our bread with the hungry and our clothing with the naked.

When my wife and I were living in Lancaster, Pennsylvania, we were in the Diocese of Harrisburg. Tithing was defined there as giving five percent to the Church and five percent to those in the community who were in need. That is the system we adopted and we still employ it.

Does this make one holy? Not in and of itself, but if we tithe we are obeying one of the laws of the Lord. Is this praiseworthy? No, again, it is simply obeying a law established by God. But why aren't our leaders enforcing this law of God by preaching it, urging it, talking about it and employing it? The leaders need to become emboldened in their leadership.

IF I FELT ANY BETTER, I WOULD BE IN HEAVEN

People love to greet one another. It is the normal, friendly, and social thing to do. A common greeting is: "How are you?" or, "How are you doing?" I try to teach a point by my response: "Any better, I'd be in Heaven!"

This statement often surprises people, or brings smiles to their faces, or causes them to chuckle. Sometimes people ask if they might adopt that response. Naturally I tell them to go right ahead and use it. I do not own those words, but it is nice of them to ask.

What do I mean by this response? It is simple: I exist, thanks to God and my parents. I can see, walk, talk, read, think, etc. I recognize that which has Beauty. All creation is beautiful in and of itself. I have friends, including my wife and children. I love the work that I do, and the work which I did for years before now. I have a great relationship with God. So I ask: What more could I ask for? Even a great abundance of money would not make me happier, nor bring me closer to the Lord.

Hence, if I felt any better, I'd be in Heaven. I have all that I need here on earth in this life. The Lord has told me many times that I will never be rich, but that I would have sufficient income and, sure enough, that has always been the case.

Anyone can adopt this approach. "But," you say, "What if someone has extremely bad health and is totally bedridden?" They might suffer from dejection, sadness, and grief. But if they recognized the value of their existence, they could see how special they are to God. The fact that they are human means that they are made in the image and likeness of God. This is something of huge value, and should be recognized. Existence *alone* gives this to people but most humans do not perceive it.

What drives me to view life and the world and my existence with joy and a sense of self-worth? Hope; which stems from and is based on Trust. Obviously my Trust and Hope is in the Lord's Word. I would likely be aimless in my life's journey, if I wasn't anchored in the Lord. My life would take paths based on low ideals: worldly values which would be of little consequence.

With my present view of life comes great joy. When you see goodness in the world and in people, you also see tremendous Beauty. All that has been created by God, no matter what it is, has great beauty in and of itself. Each thing by its very existence has inherent beauty by being what it is. This is contrary to the theory that, "Beauty is in the eye of the beholder." It should say, "Beauty is in the eye of the Creator." In other words, what God creates always has its own beauty in its existence. Remember what the book of Genesis says: after God created the world He looked at His work and saw that it was Good. All that He made is good and has beauty.

As we perceive the beauty in each thing God made, joy begins to generate in our hearts.

Allow me to relate a small journey into beauty that I experienced in the summer of 1956. While stationed at the air base in upper state New York on the western edge of Lake Champlain, I would walk half a mile to the dining hall from my work station for meals. Lake Champlain was a very long and wide lake, with Vermont on the far side.

I began to realize that I was not truly taking in my surroundings. As I walked to and fro, I began to look at the trees, and the branches on them, the new buds, and then the leaves. I looked at all these things as if I were seeing them for the first time. I looked closely. I looked at the bricks on the walls and saw, anew, the various shades of the bricks.

I saw the various patterns that the twigs and branches made as the sun glistened through the trees. I looked at the leaves and saw the various shades of green, and the intricacy of their veins carrying the life giving sap through them. I looked at the many pebbles and stones on the ground as I walked behind the buildings and trees which stood between the dirt path and the lake.

I watched the clouds drift gently with the breezes or rage across the skies ahead of an impending storm. I discovered hues and patterns that I had never seen before.

Beauty was all around me, and this planted the seeds of Joy within me.

I soon realized that if I felt any better, I would have to be in Heaven. I just needed to look at everything through the eyes of Faith to see its true existence.

The Best Goodbye

We were all born, thanks to our parents and thanks to God. Eventually we will die. Some die shortly after birth, others die long after birth. Hopefully, we will live a goodly time after our birth. And if we do (for example, I have lived for over seventy years), we watch many friends and relatives die, and hopefully go to Heaven or at least go to Purgatory for cleansing prior to continuing their journey to Heaven to spend eternity with the Lord.

Our twenty-six-year-old son Tony was killed by a drunk driver in 1996. This loss was a horrendous event and our grief was highly traumatic. The grieving never ends. Grieving is like a chameleon. This animal can change colors but the body stays the same. The body of grief stays the same but the grieving changes colors. It is still the grieving process.

My wife, our daughter Colleen, and I have grieved ever since we lost him, and we have been seeking to assist others in their own grief journeys. I have noticed that there are published books about *having no time to say goodbye* to those who die suddenly. These are the situations when the death of a loved one or friend happened so quickly that there was no time or opportunity to meet with them, to say goodbye, to tell them how much they are loved and how dear they are.

But it doesn't have to have ended that way; the best goodbye is a constant hello. When we spend time—and presence—with our loved ones and friends, we are indirectly saying goodbye. When we share presence, we are indirectly saying, "I love you." And that is what friendship is all about.

Friendships are a relationship of love, whether it be a minimal level of friendship, or the close connection of husband and wife, or that of parent and child. It is a connection of love, concern, compassion, and endearment. And when we spend time and presence with such a loved one, or friend, or acquaintance, we are indirectly saying: thanks for sharing your presence with me; I love you; I respect you; I enjoy being with you; you are special. At those times, we are indirectly saying: if you leave this life on earth, I am wishing you well on your journey to Heaven; I will miss you but at least we had pleasant times together and we loved each other, and we will be happy to again share time and presence in Heaven.

We constantly told our son Tony how special he was. We always told him how much we loved him and how great he was. We always showed our care and concern for him. A grief counselor, after Tony was killed, asked me if I wanted to say anything to him that I did not tell him while he was alive. I surprised him when I said: no. We told him, daily, how precious he was, how great he was, what a blessing he is to us, and how all who knew him felt the same way. We never stopped. We talked of normal things but we always worked into our conversations those words of praise and endearments. So, in effect, with these conversations we said our goodbyes to our son Tony, and he did the same to us.

CHILDREN ARE SPECIAL

When we hold a young child, a toddler, or even a newborn in our arms, don't we simply love them? Of course we do. They are so loveable. They need our smiles, our touch, our love and support. As they grow, they desire our encouragement and continued love and warmth. We need to take care of them, and they are grateful to us.

When I talk with friends or strangers about this, all agree that children are indeed special, even very special, and very loveable. But then I go one step further. We acknowledge that the children grow into adults. Then I ask, "Why do we no longer view them as being precious or loveable? What happens between childhood and adulthood to change our perception?"

They have no response. They are stumped.

I suggest that children lose nothing of their preciousness in becoming adults. Nor do they lose their lovability as they continue to age. We simply do not recognize it. Our "macho" mentality as adults hinders us from saying that an adult is a great and worthy person.

Using a Scripture compendium, I researched the places where "child" or "children" are mentioned and something struck me. Many places referenced the word "children." All of the citations were statements that spoke of adults, and usually multiple adults such as tribes and the Israel nation. It was not referring to toddlers or small children, but rather to persons of all ages, male and female. All of them are referred to as "children." They are the Lord's children. This is indirectly saying that all of us are God's children. Hence we are all precious persons, no matter how old we are.

Do we continue to be precious in the eyes of God? I submit that we do. We are still precious as children of God and that is how the Lord sees us—as HIS children, no matter how young or old we are in our earthly age. We were precious as children and we continue to be precious to Him.

We should respect one another as persons of great worth. God doesn't create junk. An individual can choose conduct by which he treats himself unworthily. But even unworthy conduct does not affect our true worth. God still loves us even if we disobey and go against what He teaches.

We need to show more love and respect to each other, not ignore others or be mean or indifferent to them. As brothers and sisters to one another, we need to show pleasantness and respect to everyone.

For example, we have neighbors that live near a widow. They greatly help her by planting flowers and generally assisting her with many chores, including taking meals to her. The widow has several adult children nearby but those children often ignore their mother. This helpful husband and wife are living the themes of charity and love, and are showing great respect for their widow neighbor. They do it without counting the costs.

Even if we are not willing to extend ourselves as much as these two people do, we can at least reach out to others with a pleasant greeting and, sometimes, a small helping hand. In the eyes of the Lord we are all precious. Our Creator did make each and every human being. Without that continual sustaining power of God we would all vanish in less than a second. (We should all be thankful that the Lord never has what is called a "senior moment." For the Lord's loving power sustains our existence from second to second.) This sustaining power of God shows the deep and abiding Love that the Lord has and that He shows for all of His creation.

After God created everything, the Lord looked at His creation and saw that it was good, indicating that each and every one of us, young or older, male or female, have great goodness in ourselves. That, in itself, should make us view, and treat, each other with great respect and good-will. The preciousness of each human being far exceeds all of the monetary value in the entire world. And yet we never stop to think about this, or thank the Lord for such a valuable gift. We did nothing to deserve it. Are we just as precious as the angels? I do not know. But I can say that it is the view of our Creator that we are indeed very precious and loveable. And if we are so loved unconditionally by our Creator, our God, what more do we need or want? Yes, we are human and we do seek the company and love of other humans. Hopefully such will always be part of our lives.

But we must keep in mind that we are *children* of God. When we are baptized, regardless of our age, we become children of God. We ought to act more in line with that fact. Each of us should act with more humility and gratitude for the love and care given to us by our Creator. Ought we not to act with less superiority and self-righteousness, and to treat all others with love and respect?

Getting Older

Getting older is also known as aging. I often told myself that I would "retire" at the age of ninety-five. I am seventy-seven now, and over the past three to five years my physical abilities have been deteriorating. I walk more slowly and my balance is not what it was in my youth. Age is beginning to have its effects on me.

The medical profession says that we humans will eventually live to an age of one hundred and fifty years. That has not happened yet. But it is coming. Biologists, scientists, and doctors project the age of living creatures by a formula. The age of "maturity" of any living creature is determined and this age is multiplied by the number six. The result is the projected life span of that species. That is the age they will live to under good conditions.

It has been determined that twenty-five is the age of maturity for humans. Multiply that age by six, and we have the projected life span for humans—one hundred and fifty years.

We are in the process of moving to that goal. When I was in my teens, the average life span was approximately sixty-five. It soon moved to age seventy, then seventy-five and seventy-eight. Why? We learned about nutrition, eating healthy, and adopting good exercising habits. We have begun to use good sense to become and stay healthier. Maybe we will reach our optimum by the year 2099 or 2199. But in the meanwhile, what is taking place? Our society wants the older and elderly people to live their "Golden Years" by themselves and not as part of society. It might sound harsh to say but the elderly are expected to stay out of the way of the young. I perceive an age bias, across the board, in various functions and faith groups. Years ago the adults looked upon children as those who were to be "seen and not heard." Now the elderly are viewed that way.

We older ones are thought to be non-effective, non-thinking, and non-energetic. We are expected to join senior citizen groups and to take trips and have luncheons. All that is nice but what about the elderly who want to follow the two great commandments, to love God and to love our neighbor? To love God means to serve and honor God. To love our neighbor means to serve and help our neighbors.

The expertise and abilities and love of those elderly who are presently put out to pasture, when they wish to keep serving the Lord and their neighbor, is being ignored and wasted. I went through three years of intensive training to assist in our local church parishes, along with about seventy other men and women. These non-ordained but highly trained persons were meant to assist, but very few were called upon to do so. Most were ignored and not utilized as promised.

In Pennsylvania, county judges were mandated to retire at age seventy. In 2015 it was changed to age seventy-five for mandatory retirement. This is an acknowledgment that people are living longer, that age is not necessarily a universal mark of losing abilities, and that it is senseless to waste experience, insights, and abilities. The court system could institute a case-by-case system for reviewing abilities, but that could be fraught with defects.

Our Social Security system has raised the retirement age for being able to draw from it, and there is continuing pressure to raise it even higher. The government recognizes the ability of people to live longer and to continue earning more income, which indirectly indicates that those persons still have the ability to serve others.

Our society needs to mentally "grow up" concerning their value systems about the elderly. Organizations, parishes, synagogues, charities, and committees need to view individuals as to their personal skills and abilities, especially those who wish to continue serving the Lord and their neighbors. Yes, the elderly can assist by praying for others. Prayers are indeed very powerful. But many older people can offer physical help, in addition to the power of prayer.

Throw Away Society

Forty years ago, I saw an interview on television in which an elderly man made an interesting comment that has stayed with me even to this day. The interviewer asked if he was going to throw away an item that he had used in his work but that he no longer needed. He replied that he was not. It was still able to be used, he said, so he was going to give it to a place that would rehab it and get it to someone who would put it to good use. He commented that the time and energy of other persons had gone into the making of this item and he wanted to honor them for giving part of their lives to produce it. He considered their effort as valuable and did not want to dishonor them by throwing the item away. If he threw it away, he felt he would be throwing part of the makers' lives away.

I was struck by the great respect that this man had and this stayed with me. One day we were driving down a street in Lancaster. Our children were about six and eight. It was trash collection day. I spotted a child's ukulele sitting on top of a trash can by the curb awaiting pickup by the trash truck. It looked to be in great condition so I drove around the block to get a closer look at it. I stopped the car, picked up the uke, and saw that it had one string missing. Otherwise it looked clean, in great condition, and very useable. So I took it home and further cleaned and checked it. For the next three or four years we used it, minus one string, mainly for family fun nights. Eventually I gave it to an agency that would repair it and get it to a family who would continue to have fun with it.

Now I try to recycle anything that is still useable. When we moved from Lancaster County to be near our daughter north of Philadelphia, I had to clear the house of twenty-five years of accumulation. I brought our extra possessions to a homeless shelter; they did a great job receiving things, sorting them, and selling them at their outlet store to make money for supporting themselves. Sometimes I joked that when they saw my van coming down the street they had their band come out to play a happy tune. I just kept coming and coming and coming.

We lived on the city line, and the traffic was huge. Our street was part of the system that channeled traffic around the city. Whenever I had a large item to recycle, I put it out by the curb and put a sign on it that said, "FREE: Just Take It."

Every time I put such an item out, someone took it the same day. One time our neighbor had a large and very heavy grill he wanted to give away. He and I hauled it to the curb after I persuaded him to try my method. I put the signs on it. In a day it was gone. Somebody in a car saw it, stopped to look it over, drove off, and within an hour came back in a pickup truck with another person. The neighbor and I helped them lift it onto the truck, and they drove off with it.

On another occasion, we helped our daughter move to an apartment when she got a teaching job at a high school about sixty miles away from Lancaster. She had a workable microwave oven that she didn't need anymore. So I took it out to the curb and went to make a sign, but by the time I got back down to the curb, the microwave was gone.

As I drive along the streets, I often spot good items being put out for trash pickup. It's so wasteful when the items appear to have a remaining useable life. People just do not care, or do not want to take a bit of time to locate a place that will take it. One time we gave a bed to an Asian family by phoning the church group who was sponsoring them. It doesn't take long to do these things.

If people are willing to recycle glass and plastic bottles and cardboard and newspapers, why aren't they self-imposing a like discipline to recycle useable larger items such as chairs, bureaus, sofas, and beds?

Such discipline would develop great qualities and values in people, like compassion, care, generosity, kindness, and concern for the people in need. Additionally it would develop insights, such as the need for better education, for equitable distributions, greater visions in governments, and employment opportunities.

The people of this nation must stop being such wasteful humans. Respect must become a cornerstone of our dealings with people and with things.

Pray Always, and If Necessary, Use Words

How can a very busy person "pray always"? It seems that this is an impossible task! People have households to maintain, jobs to accomplish, income to earn, leisure to employ, sleep to achieve, procreation to accomplish, etc. With all of this to accomplish within a twenty-four-hour day, we are fortunate to say even a few prayers a day. And yet some urge us to *pray always*!

A very prayerful person named Augustine lived in northern Egypt in the fourth and fifth century. We now know him as Saint Augustine. I believe that *pray always* was attributed to him.

So what did he urge people to do to accomplish this? Well, when we pray to God, we show a loving relationship with the Lord. This relationship grows stronger as we continue to pray. We move closer and closer to Him so that eventually it is as if the two of us have become one.

How do we accomplish it? Augustine said that the answer is *desire*. A desire for the Lord is a silent prayer coming from the heart. And if we desire Him always, then we are praying always. When I first met my wife, I began to desire to date her and so we went out together. We spent time together to learn to know each other. As we did, I desired to spend more and more time and presence with her. We had more frequent and longer dates.

This desire kept developing and growing stronger until the two of us became one by our marriage. Our desire for each other's love had reached its goal by our joining together as one. We have spent our lives together in love and in prayer. We have become as one in love. In love as in prayer, we desire to be with the one we seek. We desire to be with the one we love. We desire to communicate with the one we love. Prayer is a form of communication. Prayer is also an act of love whether verbal or non-verbal. Either way, it is a desire to be present, one to the other, in a sharing of the hearts.

In prayer, we want to be with God. If we don't feel close to Him but still desire Him, then the prayer grows stronger as the yearning deepens and grows. Anguish develops from the separation. Yearning draws us to seek Him whose presence we miss. Joy returns when we get closer and closer to Him.

This is the way it is with us and God. There are similarities in how it is with my wife Bernadette and me. In marriages where the man and woman are in love with each other and with God who is forming their union, such love is not simply carnal. It is also a desire to aid and assist the other in their communications with God, Who seeks their permanent good.

My wife and I were conceived, grew, were born, became adults, grew older, and eventually will die and be buried. Our souls will go to Heaven (by the grace of God) and eventually our bodies will rise again to be rejoined with our souls in Heaven for all eternity. This faith and hope helps to guide our lives.

We can communicate with God through prayer and God communicates with us as well as with all of His creation, in multitudinous and various ways.

Many people seek and pray for guidance as to various things and activities in their lives. Many times I have sought guidance for direction in my life. Decisions had to be made. I had to choose to do some activity or not, so I prayed for guidance. The answers came. They came usually in words. Sometimes they came much later. But the responses came in words. Sometimes I overheard people talking and some words they spoke seemed to stick in my mind. These words turned out to be the answers to my quest for directions.

Another time I was at a presentation being given by a nun we knew. As she presented her thoughts by reading her script, I was struck by some of the words. Afterwards I asked if I could read part of her papers. I found the words and knew that this was the answer to my prayers.

Does everyone seeking direction in their lives get the answers in this fashion? Of course not. The Lord communicates however He wants but this was how He dealt with me.

But the Lord communicates with each and every soul who seeks Him and seeks aid and direction. The Lord is the greatest and best communicator ever. God doesn't create junk. God's creation is always good. God loves all of what He created. And love is the highest form of communication. God loves His creation immensely. This means that God communicates with all of us immensely and constantly.

So have hope. Have trust. Have faith that your prayer requests will be heard and answered—but always in God's time and manner. The answers may not always be what we expect. They will be what God knows we need or what is best for us.

I once knew a lady employed at our bank in Lancaster. They told her that she would be laid off due to downsizing. She asked me to pray for her that she would not be let go. She was laid off anyway, and appeared devastated. I continued to pray for her. Within a very short time she was hired in the county court system. She thrived in this responsible job and learned many new skills.

So remember: Pray always, and if necessary, use words.

Tempus Fugit; Memento Mori

This is one of the best phrases to keep in mind. Translated from the Latin, it means: Time flies; Remember death. *Memento mori* means that we ought to keep in mind that we must die. When? We do not know. But our mortal and earthly life will end. Of this we are absolutely certain.

In medieval days, people were reminded often about their mortality. It was a practice to keep in mind the vanity of earthly life and the transient nature of earthly goods and pursuits.

Since then ascetic disciplines have helped perfect one's character by cultivating "detachment" from things. This line of thought also is a means of developing other virtues and not just detachment. It helps us to remember the immortality of one's soul and the afterlife.

In medieval times, this phrase helped people to realize the fleetingness of earthly pleasures, luxuries, and achievements; it taught that people should rather focus on the afterlife and strongly consider where one wishes to spend one's eternal existence after death—Heaven or Hell.

People in our country do not often consider that we do not live forever and that our days on earth are limited. Life is like a lit candle and eventually the candle burns down and the light goes out. But we did not purchase the candle and we do not know the length of it nor the burn time for this particular candle. We also cannot predict unexpected events such as a sudden rain storm or a strong wind, which can extinguish the light in an untimely way.

Hence, how appropriate is the phrase, "Tempus fugit; Memento mori."

It is such a tragedy when a person wastes the precious gem of their life. I felt very sad when this happened to someone I knew. I represented this young man one time in criminal court. The police and I knew he was a drug user. He was in his mid-thirties. Unfortunately he overdosed one night and died. A police officer I knew joked about his death. He smiled and said that we will not be bothered by him anymore. But I was saddened by it; this young man had wasted something very precious: his own life. When I said this to the officer, he understood, and his manner changed from levity to sadness.

Obviously the drug user, had seldom, if ever, given any thought to this phrase. He chose to live for the moment only, and it backfired for him. In any case, I was terribly saddened by his waste of his life, and unfortunately I watched many others do similar self-destructive things in harming themselves and destroying their lives.

There are many styles of self-destructiveness and wasteful behavior. I see so much potential in people but they do not develop it. Everyone has so many abilities and yet people do not seek to explore what these are. If they do recognize some such abilities lying in wait, they do little or nothing to develop this potential, even if they have the free time to accomplish it.

Tempus fugit; Memento mori.

Peer Pressure

When I was a young boy, it seemed that everyone in our neighborhood had set values. The simplest ones were, for example, to not steal, to respect the elderly, to offer to assist the disabled or elderly if they needed it, to show consideration to others, and similar values. These principles were established and held in place by peer pressure. A person who violated them was chastised by others around them. They were generally instilled by the approval, or disapproval, given by the community.

People communicated, neighbors to neighbors, and expressed their views and values to each other. If neighbors acted in accord with the right values, they were praised, and if not, they were indirectly scolded and talked about.

Naturally, most people adhered to and acknowledged the existence and applicability of the Ten Commandments. Parents instilled value systems in their children and indirectly in their neighborhoods by talking of general values.

But nowadays, such community discussions have mainly faded away. People are reluctant and afraid to share their ideas and talk values with their neighbors. In fact it would appear that people are afraid to even speak with their neighbors. The peer pressures have reversed and seem to be presently stuck in reverse, like a car going the wrong way.

Over the years many varied social-value systems and the ideas of such systems have crept into the thinking of our societies. Hence many competing ways of thinking have developed. There is nothing wrong with having a multitude of various and competing social-value systems. Neighborhood discussions could, and should, take place. In fact, discussions would bring better understanding. For example, many in our "over 55" community are single persons, widows or widowers, and many live with persons of the opposite gender, without the benefit of marriage. Should that take place? They do not know except they desire it and so they do it. But no one talks about it, except in private with maybe one or two persons. No one discusses it with the persons involved or with their neighbors. People fear talking and discussing such lifestyles.

The response would be, "It is none of your business." But it is their business. Community and neighborly values are the business of others around them. If a neighborhood husband beats up the wife once or twice a week, shouldn't it be talked about or even reported to the police? Community values are the business of the communities.

But this is not happening. People are fearful of expressing themselves openly. An *I* mentality crept into society—such as *I* am like a "god" and *I* will do as *I* decide to do. *I* will not share anything with anyone. *I* am in charge and no one will change *me* nor tell *me* what to think or do. *I* am supreme. Everyone else is less worthy than *me*.

This dangerous mentality inhibits a sharing of thoughts. When we were in school we grew and developed by sharing and evaluating and discerning. We ought to continue maturing rather than stalling out and coming to a halt. By developing an *I* mentality we push away family and friends. We end up with closed minds, which have the social effect of being like rivers, lakes, and seas which dry up and have all life therein cease.

Open sharing, instead, is compared to healthy rain water causing hydration. Open discussions and respectful sharing insure development and healthy growth.

Tunnel Vision

When a person looks ahead, they usually see at a width of 180 degrees, from one side to the other. But in a tunnel, the field of vision narrows. The sides begin to collapse towards the center. As you drive through a long tunnel, you cannot see very far on either side because the side walls limit your views. You look straight ahead and wish that you might soon see the light at the end of the tunnel which shows that your tunnel journey will soon come to an end.

I knew I had to develop tunnel vision as I approached adult life. As my wonderful mother often put it, she and my father didn't have two nickels to rub together. Financially they just kept their heads above water and were always on the verge of going under and financially drowning.

If I were to get a college education and go further, I would have to earn my own money to succeed. So, in the military I earned nearly two years of college credits by taking evening courses on base. With God's blessings I was able to transfer those credits to a college of my choice when I left the military. But I had to work summers and nights in order to finish college.

While I was in the service, I met a young lady that I got along with very well. But I knew that if I married and had children, I would not succeed at marriage and college both at the same time. When leaving the military at age twenty-three, I felt that I had to concentrate on education. I focused on work and school, knowing that I had to do that in order to get where I wanted to be. I wanted a degree and the possibility of proceeding towards a further degree, maybe in law. And so I adopted a "tunnel vision" for my life's goals.

I had known several people who said they wished to become lawyers. I took part in some of their discussions as to what lawyers do. I read some books about Clarence Darrow, who was a nationally-known American trial lawyer who took on society-changing cases such as the Scopes Monkey Trial case, which dealt with whether evolution or Biblical creation should be taught in public schools.

When I finished college I decided to enter law school. But money, or the lack thereof, forced me to take a year away from this goal, and I got a low-skill job to earn money for my continued education. At that time a year of education did not cost as much as it does today. People could nearly "pay as you go" for higher education.

When I entered law school I continued the same process of work and study. Three years later I became a lawyer. I could then broaden my vision to other pursuits, such as marriage, family, house, car, vacations, etc.

The tunnel vision disappeared. It had served its purpose. Life became easier with much less pressure. I could now see sunshine in my life since I had passed through that long, long tunnel.

Was it easy getting to these goals? Naturally not. But there was no other way. I didn't mind (too much) spending some years working, or working during the school years while others were out having fun. If I wanted to get to these goals, there was no choice. The stress of this journey was high. But once I became a lawyer, I knew that this was highly satisfying work. I might have chosen to be a physician, but the financial demands to get there were beyond me.

In my law practice I concentrated on serving the poor and low-income clients. I knew what they were going through. In effect I had lived that lifestyle as I worked my way through the education process. My tunnel vision served me well and I was able to practice law for the next thirty years. After that I turned to church ministry as a lay ecclesial minister, after getting a master's degree at night school in philosophy.

So if you have a dream you strongly wish to pursue, then you need to have the means to achieve it. You need to be willing to commit the time to achieve it with patience and a great commitment. Best wishes to you to achieve your goals! They are reachable.

Plan well. Execute your plans well. Persevere and stay committed. If your goals are worthy ones, then persist and do not let them drift away. Maybe you cannot take giant steps towards reaching them, but take the small ones and continue on the journey. Even if the steps falter or temporarily stop, just restart and continue. Persist and persist. If family matters cause the journey to end, just remember that family comes first.

Too Much, Too Much, Too Much

One day while my wife was grocery shopping, I tried a small experiment in the supermarket meat section. I stood back and looked up and down the entire length of the meat, cheese, and fish sections. I looked and looked and looked at all of the varieties and packs of products. I was amazed—literally amazed—at so many choices for would-be purchasers.

When we went to other supermarkets, I did the same thing but in various food sections. I simply stood back and looked up and down the aisles, viewing all of the varieties available of sodas, crackers, cereals, canned vegetables, fresh vegetables, paper products, etc. I saw a huge variety of similar foods and products available for purchasing by the American people.

What would it be like if America again suffered a huge depression? Many would be out of work and much of people's savings would simply vanish or be greatly reduced in size. What then?

What would become of this grossly huge variety of food stuffs?

Even without a depression, the real question is: Do we need all of this? Do we need all these varieties for the same basic generic products? Do we need all the varieties of junk food? Do we even need all of the varieties of basic life-sustaining foods?

Some might say that such is "free enterprise" and producers should be free to make what they hope to sell. They also say that Americans are better off with such great varieties to select from.

I like to answer the way that the American soldiers answered in the Second World War when the German troops surrounded them and asked if they wish to surrender. They replied: "Nuts!"

We have an overabundance of things in this country: in the food industry, the automotive industry, television makers, etc. This overabundance is not needed nor, realistically, is it desired by Americans.

I pray that we could give much of our abundance to areas of the world where there is a dearth of any similar goods, even right here in our own nation. Many people live in poverty or near poverty, here or other countries, especially in Central and South America and other Third World countries. How great it would be for us to help raise the standard of living for such people, without creating "dependent nations"!

What if we could buy some of the overabundance and give them to people in great need? Or train people how to make and produce such goods? This could be done as part of our tithing, giving to the poor under the mechanism of tithing.

The best place to start this is in your neighborhood. You do not always have to think of areas overseas even though those are the most desperate. Many in this country can truthfully use a helping hand to assist them. Some would simply be taking advantage of your generosity but most are in real need of your generous and caring gifts of time and material help.

Needs are in varying degrees, great or small. My wife and I honeymooned in Puerto Rico. We rented a car to see the island. But the roads did not lend themselves to doing it, so we only drove around one-fourth of the island. Coming through the forests in the northeast we saw much abject poverty.

I became aware that poverty can greatly vary, and I understood why so many people from that island were moving to the United States in the 1950s. Poverty in the United States was far better than the poverty in Puerto Rico; it was much better to be poor in the United States than in many other places in this world.

So pick and choose where to give. But above all—give, help, assist. We have so much need to be compassionate and loving and giving and caring in helping our brothers and sisters in their needs, without counting the costs.

Hello Young Man; Hello Young Lady

Sometimes when I use such a greeting with an older person, they are confused. One time I said such a greeting to a very elderly man, and he became upset. I suspect that he thought I was ridiculing him, but I wasn't. Usually I get a return "hello" or a smile or even a "thank you." I use that greeting with nearly everyone.

If the person responds in a way that invites conversation, I try to develop one. The person often says that they wish they were young again. And I insist that they are. I then explain the secret to being young, even when they have lived for a good many years.

I ask them if they have a soul. They say that they do. They admit that their body is getting older and that they have more aches and pains. Perhaps they are losing some abilities or slowing down or their balance is not as it used to be. Indirectly they admit that their body is going downhill.

They then admit that their body is mortal but their soul is immortal. Once they admit these two aspects—a mortal body and an immortal soul—I then urge them to live by their immortal soul and not by their body. I urge them to live with the joy of life which comes from their soul, which never grows old. Hence, if their soul doesn't age, neither do they. They should ignore, as best they can, their body with the aches and pains.

Pain is pain and loss is loss, and a chronic condition is often difficult to deal with, but there is joy in living. Life itself is a joy and the process of life—living—is capable of one joy after the other. A life of joy can be long lasting, like having a wonderful marriage, or the joy which comes from one's children, or having a job that is enjoyed very much, or having friends whose company is a joy. All are great examples of sources of joy in a person's life.

Living to old age can be a joy if one is mainly anchored in one's soul and if one practices acceptance of one's pain and discomfort and deterioration of bodily abilities. The trick is to live by the guidance of one's immortal soul.

Since God has created us, and our soul, He is anchoring us in His life and filling us with His graces. We thereby have a source to draw upon of unending joy in our lives.

Our soul is where God abides. He gives us His peace, endurance, consolation, understanding, patience, and wisdom. If we can draw upon these great gifts, we can be eternally young despite our bodies' aches and pains.

Our bodies can lose physical abilities. My balance is becoming not-so-good. I walk much more slowly and I use walking sticks. But that is okay. I am as I am. I am alive: walking, talking, sharing presence with family and friends, and being active in various church ministries. I accept what I am and who I am. But there is joy in all of this since I strive to live from my soul as a driving force of life. God is the source of all of our lives, including mine.

Poverty

The number of families and individuals living below the poverty level in the United States, according to national statistics, is stunning. A family is considered to be living in poverty if their income falls below a certain annual amount. In 2009 the poverty level in the United States was $21,831 gross annual income for a family of four with two children aged seventeen or younger. This was the poverty line, although at that time the majority of Americans believed that it took at least $35,000 annually to adequately take care of a family of four.

In the year 2010 there were over thirty-nine million Americans living below the national poverty level. In 2007 there were thirty-seven million in the United States living in poverty and in 2008 this grew to slightly over thirty-nine million.

We can translate this into the number of families living in poverty. Per the United States Census Bureau, in 2008, out of 77.9 million families there were 8.15 million families living in poverty. This was 10.3 percent higher than in 2007.

Of course this refers to people living in the United States. When Bernadette and I were in Puerto Rico and rented a car, we drove east, then south down the coast, then turned west about midway down the island, before going north back to our hotel. We witnessed the abject poverty of the people living in the country area. We saw a one room "house" built on stilts, with a ladder to the door. Multiple families lived in this one room, with a large area cut out of the center of the floor that the people used as a latrine.

But here in our own country, a large part of the population exists in poverty, and even more importantly, many live in poverty of spirit. By this I mean the lack of spirituality: the lack of religious spirit which exists in the people in this country. This includes adults and children, men and women, educated and non-educated. More and more are falling below the poverty level in spirituality, more quickly than in the area of economic poverty. Some accept and adhere to a faith belief and individually pray and believe, but not in an in-depth manner.

In this type of poverty, the knowledge of God is often non-existent or simply a roadblock which needs to be avoided. They live a very materialistic existence. Some have a value system in place which was established in their youth, but these systems can change and are insecurely anchored. Others live by no value system at all.

We should fear a person who is totally devoid of values. It is a frightening experience to encounter such a person.

As an attorney, I defended many accused persons. One young defendant was in his mid-twenties. His parents had never instilled any value system, or any principles whatsoever. He never spoke in terms of anything being right or wrong; all things to him simply "were." He had no thought that some conduct might be right or wrong, good or bad. He was a hollow shell of a person. In other words, he was someone to be feared and avoided. He was a living vacuum.

Such persons are somewhat rare. Usually godless persons have some type of good/bad, right/wrong, fair/unfair mentality as part of their lives.

But when you engage them in conversations about God, or fairness, or justice, or good/bad, they talk in scattered and non-cohesive language. They do not assert any basis for their ideas, or why they do what they do, or why others would act as they do. Their thoughts about an afterlife are as wispy as smoke rising upwards into the wind. If they believe in an afterlife, they offer no basis to justify seeking it.

I wonder why they are lacking such a vision, and why they do not question and wonder about the existence of God and of themselves and the relationship between God and themselves. Why do they not have an active curiosity to explore their relationship between these two most valuable entities? Have Americans lost the sense of wonder?

Do they not question why they exist, or what happens after they die, or whether there is good or bad conduct in life, or what will happen after death if they live a very bad life? Where is their questioning and how do they search for answers? Do they answer their questions simply *ipse dixit*? Do they simply state an answer based on whatever thought pops into their mind, even if it has no basis in reality other than its presence in their mind? Even children in the first grade of school can do better than that.

So why not search out answers based in reality? It might present a challenge and take some time and effort, but many of these questions and answers are worthy of such efforts.

Marriage Between Persons of the Same Gender

The United States Supreme Court has issued a ruling that it was a constitutional right for persons of the same gender to become married to each other. The Court has, by its slim margin of five to four, made legal a falsehood. They have taken what for some was a friendship and established, in law, what can only be a myth of falseness.

People cannot deny that Scripture exists. In the Pentateuch, the third book contains a set of laws given by God to Moses at Mount Sinai. The book of Leviticus is almost legislative in character. These laws taught the Jews (and, by extension, Christians) that they are always to keep themselves in a state of purity and sanctity. This would become a sign of their intimate union with God, especially when the Lord instructed the people to be holy because He, the Lord, is Holy.

The Israelites had lived a long time in Egypt. At first, when there was a great famine across the entire area where the Israelites and many others lived, the only place where much grain was stored and available, was in Egypt. Joseph, an Israelite, was entrusted by Pharaoh with the charge of giving people enough grain to survive. This included anyone who came and asked for it. Joseph's brothers and father moved to Egypt, and many Israelites came to stay and settle in Egypt. In fact, they greatly multiplied while living there. They grew so much that the Egyptians feared that the Israelites might take over as a ruling class.

The Israelites had acquired many of the customs of the Egyptians. They became like the Egyptians in many of their lifestyles, except their religious faith practices. When they fled from Egypt they moved back to the land of their origin and heritage but carried with them the lifestyle of the Egyptians. But the Lord did not want that in the land of promise. So the book of Leviticus came into existence to re-teach God's people how to rightly live.

One should read the entire book to get the sense of how detailed it is. For example, it explains clean and unclean food, whether it be of insects, fish, or animals. It spells out what could or could not be eaten. It explains how to deal with cleanliness after childbirth, leprosy of the body, and the clothes worn or houses lived in during illness. It spells out personal uncleanliness and the specialness of sexual relations, and with whom such relations could or couldn't take place. It deals with respecting strangers, and forbids worshipping false gods, stealing, defrauding, and hating others.

Obviously, while in Egypt, the people had learned wrong ways of living and they needed to be told how to return to the proper way. This book had tremendous influence on all of the lifestyles in the Middle East, and then on Europe and the Western ways of life. I am surprised that no scholar has tried to show how much this book influenced millions of peoples and cultures through the ages.

Chapter eighteen sets forth the sanctity of sex. It reflects on the fact that the Israelites had lived amongst the Egyptians and their customs of living, and had been enslaved there. Yet when they were freed from slavery, God had to teach them to break away from the ways that were wrong.

For example, a son was forbidden to have sexual intercourse with his mother. It was forbidden with his father's wife, with the daughters of the father or mother, with the daughter of a son or daughter of his, and so on. We can say that this is common sense but this "common sense" came from the book of Leviticus in the Pentateuch, contained in the Bible.

Leviticus condemns any practice of sexual relations of a human with an animal. Nor is a male to have sexual relations with another male as he would with a woman. Such conduct is called an abomination. And the use of the word "male," at that time, also referred to a woman, so that sexual conduct of a woman with a woman was also forbidden.

This book of the Bible is full of such laws for the conduct of human life. Such rules became the heritage for how humans were to live. And once instituted as a way of human life, it was an impossibility for any theory of separation of Church and State to have eliminated such ways of living from humanity. This conduct was then anchored into societies and formed the basis of "common sense."

It is perhaps good that the penalties set forth in this book are not the laws of this nation of ours. For in chapter twenty it is set forth that if a man lies with a male as with a woman, both of them will be put to death for their abominable deed.

Many will say that these writings are old and, as such, out of date and no longer applicable. But it's obvious that the rules for conduct set forth in Leviticus are the source for the life rules which we follow and which our society continues to adhere to and follow.

God never goes out of date. God never loses His authenticity nor His validity. His teachings and rules and laws never lose validity or authority for all of humankind. God is the only One Who has authority to change His rules.

For those who do not believe in God we ask, "Does common sense go out of date?" Of course not. Common sense is always relevant.

The United States Supreme Court has caused a rift in our society. Our society is now fractured and broken. Many, like myself, will never accept this decision. Like the Dred Scott decision of years past, it is humanly wrong in its substance. It is not "true." It is not a valid decision based on the metaphysics of humans. I will always accept and respect other people, but I will never accept that a male is married to another male. Likewise no female can ever be truly and validly married to another female. The law says it is legal for such to be married to each other. But it is a living lie and falsehood. I respect such individuals. Such will never diminish my respect for them as God's creatures, for it is in itself wrong to hate any person. It is obvious that such persons have deep and abiding friendships. But they do not have a true and valid marriage despite what the law says.

And so all I can say is: God bless America. And: God help America.

Singing in Church

During Protestant services, the attending faithful sing strongly and forthrightly. They do not hold back since they are praising the Lord for all that He does for them.

But in a Roman Catholic church, during Mass, singing is absolutely not the parishioners' strong suit. The singing is quiet or nearly non-existent. Maybe only God can understand why.

A Catholic once said that if you pray, you pray just once. But when you sing, you are praying twice. Maybe we should extend that one more step and say that when you sing strongly, you are praying three times.

When the subject of singing arises I often urge Catholics to sing like a Protestant—that is, to sing with vigor. In church, I am often in the rear but singing strongly enough that the people in the sanctuary can hear me and know who is singing. Why not? Shouldn't we be sure that the Lord knows that we are there and are praising Him?

Why are so many people afraid to tell God how precious He is to them? Singing is a human activity which shows the joy in our hearts. Why are people so hesitant to communicate how much we love God and others?

It doesn't matter if one cannot sing well. God sees our hearts and maybe God is tone deaf (well, okay, not really). But the Lord wants us to speak, and sing, our love to Him. God has made so many different types of humans. God will take us as we are, and not wait for us to become as we would like to be (which may never happen in our lifetime on earth).

Praying thrice (singing strongly), or even twice (singing), or even once (just praying), is all that the Lord is asking of us. He doesn't ask for a great deal. He doesn't make us all outstanding singers. He only gives such gifts to a few, but He loves us just as we are. The Lord simply wants us to communicate with Him.

The best way to do that is to pray thrice. I suspect that the Lord is wishing for the Roman Catholics to begin praying that way. (I know I am.)

We tell, and show, our children or parents just how precious they are to us. Such enthusiasm is hard to hold back. It is the same when we show our spouse how much we love. We don't hesitate to let our enthusiasm run loose and strong.

Sometimes we feel like shouting our love from the rooftops. So why not do the same for God?

Quiet times are precious too; they allow us to hear what the Lord is trying to tell us. There is a time and place for everything. A time for quiet. A time for praying thrice. If we want to be quiet all or most of the time, then maybe we should enter a monastery to talk to the Lord in that setting.

Communication is very important. During the process of Marriage Encounter,[4] we instruct engaged couples that communication between married people is an extremely important part of building a lasting relationship. With that in mind, ought we not communicate often with our Creator since it is He who holds everything in existence at all times? Having received such a great gift as our existence, we ought to constantly thank and praise our Creator.

---

[4] Marriage Encounter is a process of advising engaged couples as to what they can expect in their marriages, and what they ought to consider doing to strengthen their relationships with each other.

Beware—Devils Do Exist

Many humans act as if the devil and his cohorts do not exist. If they do acknowledge their existence, they act as if the devils are far, far away and do not interact with humans.

But beware: they do exist, and they roam throughout the earth, constantly seeking to entice us to fall into their traps. They try to get us to act against the eternal precepts for holiness.

Satan and his workers are well practiced in the art of deception. They have been around much longer than humans. They have been practicing their art of deceit all of that time. I would highly suspect that before humans came to exist, they attempted to entice fellow angels to leave Heaven and join them. They are well accustomed to deceiving others and they love to work on us weaker ones called humans, especially knowing that we are children of God.

They know our nature and they know our weaknesses. They spend time with us to slyly get us away from the road to holiness.

Our Creator allows us to be tempted. By fighting temptations, we prove that we do indeed want to be with God in Heaven for eternity. Maybe it is God's way to see that we do, in fact, deserve to spend eternity with Him. After all, we read in Scripture how the Lord put many to the test. Jacob wrestled all night with an angel. It ended in a draw. The Lord changed his name from Jacob to Israel.

Earlier, Abram was put to a great test of trust and faith. God, through an angel, instructed him to place his only son on an altar of wood and put his son to death. As Abram was about to do as he was asked, God's angel stopped him and substituted a goat for the sacrifice.

The greatest test was with the devil and Jesus Himself. Our Lord had spent forty days in the desert in prayer and fasting. He was extremely weak and hence the most vulnerable, and the devil sought to entice Jesus to abandon the Father and worship the devil. Jesus won this test of faith, three times, and we must do the same.

We are often put to the test. At school, we are tested and prove ourselves worthy by passing. We grow and develop by being tested. This is how we progress in school and grow in knowledge. God does the same with us. When you get into stressful or disturbing life situations, God may be putting you into the crucible to test your faith resolve. If we pray, we will grow in our faith and trust in the Lord by such tests.

Keep in mind what Scripture says of God-given trials. For example, in James 1:2-4, we read:

My brothers, count as pure joy when you are involved in every sort of trial. Realize that when your faith is tested, this makes for endurance. Let endurance come to its perfection so that you may be fully mature and lacking in nothing.

Be strong. Avoid temptation. Avoid Satan and his workers. Pray. Talk with God often and always. And did I mention to pray, pray, pray?

Saint Teresa of Avila, in some of her great writings, said that one way to chase away a bothering temptation from devils is the use of Holy Water. They cannot stand Holy Water. Don't forget to seek help from the saints and angels.

One time in church awaiting the start of Mass, I was greatly attacked with evil thoughts by a devil. I prayed to Saint Michael the Archangel to chase the devil away. He answered my prayers, and within seconds the temptations ended.

Don't be fooled by a carrot dangling from a string at the end of a stick. This old trick gets a horse, harnessed to a wagon, to move forward and pull the heavy wagon. The carrot for us is an enticement, used by the devil. It is used to induce us to rouse our desires, whether it is for wealth, lust, power, pride, status, glory or whatever else appeals to us. The devil uses this "carrot" to get us to move towards it and thus move the "wagon" forward. The wagon is a symbol of some type of sin that moves us away from the Lord. Some enticements even start from our own bad habits which we have personally and willfully developed.

There are other and more severe possessions by demons controlling humans, but such are rare. Be assured that demons cannot ever *own* any person since we belong to God alone.

Yet we have many defenses against the devils. One of the best aids is prayer. Turn to prayer during any temptation or any time in need. Continue with prayer even when not in temptation. Prayer is a direct communication with the Lord. Allow prayer to give praise to God, or thank Him, or ask Him for special needs, or simply talk with God. Ask for guidance and not just for deliverance.

Our Enemy Is the Devil

The epistle of James (4:1-7) lists three ongoing spiritual battles we have in our earthly lives, namely, with the world, the flesh, and the devil. Many dismiss the devils' existence as outdated superstitions. Therefore many know very little about them.

A small book entitled *Manual for Spiritual Warfare,* by Paul Thigpen, is a great resource for getting to know more about the devils and how to combat them. Its information and insights would be greatly useful for all faith-filled persons.

Jesus referred to demons several times. Scriptures refer to the casting out of demons by Jesus and His Apostles on many occasions. Satan is their leader and he and his devils were originally good angels who rebelled against God and were expelled from Heaven. Each has an intellect, free will, and knowledge. But they are still created entities.

God allows the devils to try to distract us humans and get us to join their ranks and leave the Lord. Pray that we will not do that.

The devils seek to create doubts in our beliefs. Even if we know the truth about our faith and have good understanding, they seek to plant doubts in us, especially in our choice of worthy actions and making good decisions. They are especially artful in making wrong actions appear enticing and good, or at least "not wrong." Such thoughts appear as our own even though the source might be from a devil.

They are extremely adept at deception. That is why it is beneficial for us to know what is right and what is wrong, so that we may continue to practice good conduct. By doing this we develop our virtues.

Virtues are habits of good and proper conduct. By such practice of right conduct it becomes easier and easier to make right choices time and again. Virtue consists of habits created by good actions done over and over.

The devils seek to cause doubts in us, especially as to our faith understanding. Take for example questions we might have: Does God really exist? How do we know that God exists? Is there a Heaven? If there is, how do I get there since I am a weak human?

Prayer, study of Scripture, trust, faith and belief, and Mass and the sacraments will give the answers. The surest way to achieve your place in Heaven is to follow the Way that Jesus taught.

Holiness

Only God is holy. No human, in and of himself, is holy. By our efforts alone we cannot achieve even a drop of holiness. And yet we seek holiness. Is it achievable? The road to holiness is simple to find. Walking that road can be extremely easy or extremely difficult depending on our life values and what we desire to achieve. It all depends on us as individuals.

The first chapter of Genesis tells us that we are made in the image and likeness of God. Does that make us holy? I would say that it does, in a sense, except for the fall of Adam and Eve.

But what do we mean when we say that we are made in the image and likeness of God? Further on in Scripture, it states that we are children of God. All children are very similar to and "like" their parents. But like all children we need to develop, grow and mature, in all aspects of our humanness, including holiness. We need to know that we are in the image of God and that we are children of God. Our human parents have not been doing a very good job of teaching us that in our childhood. In fact, even in our adult life we do not know that very often.

Hence, since God alone is holy, and He has taught us how to live and to achieve Heaven so as to be with Him for all eternity, then the obvious way to achieve holiness is to follow God's teachings as to how to live. Following the Way that the Lord has shown to all of us who are, or who were, or who are yet to come, is the simple road that leads to holiness and, eventually, to Paradise where we will be eternally holy.

In the early years of Christianity the people were not referred to as Christians. Instead, Christianity was simply referred to as "The Way." It was simply seen as the road to God, as the road to Paradise. The Way to live, as taught by Jesus the Christ, was known as The Way to achieve life in Heaven and to be with God for all eternity. Jesus said that what He taught was given to Him by His Father, and when He ascended into Heaven, He left us the Paraclete: the Holy Spirit, to assist us on The Way.

Saint Paul often tells us in his letters that he was no longer living his life. Instead he was living the life of the Lord. In other words, Paul was living the life of Jesus. Paul was still Paul but he was not doing as he, Paul, willed to do but as Jesus wanted Paul to live and do. Paul was following The Way. Now Paul had a little extra help since Jesus was speaking to him directly at times, as implied in Scripture. But we have similar help from the Holy Spirit and all we have to do is to read the Scriptures and to follow The Way.

So why not take the road to Holiness? In the 1500s there was a nun who lived in Avila, Spain. She was a prolific writer of spiritual books. In one of them she wrote that when we compare ourselves to God, we are as nothing—or even less than nothing. God is so great, so powerful, so full of goodness, so knowledgeable, He is beyond measure. The Lord simply cannot be gauged nor measured in any aspect. Compared with Him, we humans are small, inept, and sunk in nothingness.

Yet as Scripture tells us, we are so very special as God's adopted children. Now we are extremely weak, dependent, sinful people. Compared to God we are as nothing. But in Heaven, we will be enhanced and glorified. For as Saint Paul intimated, eye has not seen nor has ear heard what we shall be. We have sure and secure trust that our Heavenly Father, who sustains us on our earthly journey, will love us and treat us as His beloved sons and daughters, like the saints and angels.

Does a father dismiss or ignore his children? Does a father hate his children? Or does a father love and "adore" his children? Does not a father hover over his children to care for and protect them? Does not a father give up all to provide for his children?

We look to our future existence with well-founded trust, hope, and great anticipation to have a joyous existence. I personally long to be reunited with our son who was killed by an intoxicated driver when he was twenty-six. I miss him greatly and the grieving process never gets any easier.

But as the years pass, I also recognize that I greatly miss the presence of Jesus, and His Father, and the Holy Spirit. Yes, their presence is with us in various ways but we long to have human type of contact with them—face-to-face. Moses asked the Lord to be able to see Him face-to-face and that was granted to him.

I also miss the uncles, aunts, relatives, friends, and acquaintances that have touched my heart with their love and presence over the years. I miss them so much and am anxious to again be present with them. They are such gifts of joy. How we long, with desire, for that joy.

But should I end my own life so as to hurry my presence with them? If I did, would I be guaranteed that such will happen? No. Why not? I do not "own" my own life. Why not? Because our lives are gifts from our Creator—from God. Our existence is given to us by God. Our continued existence, day after day, second after second, is

His gift to us. God gives, and God alone has the right to take away.

Someone asked, "Whose life is it anyway?" in a situation of medical euthanasia. The simple and indisputable answer is that our lives belong solely to the Lord—and not to us. We thus have no right of self-destruction, and if we have no right of self-destruction we therefore have no right to take the life of any other human being. Doing so would destroy our road to holiness.

Spreading the Good News

Four thousand years have elapsed since the days of Abraham, Isaac, Jacob (Israel), and Joseph. Moses came later, and many others followed, including King David and the other prophets. Jesus came and taught us, and years later the Gospels were written and promulgated. His disciples and Apostles gave us the Epistles. Various leaders have since given us reflections and teachings based on this heritage. All of this can be referred to as *The Good News*. But many limit that phrase to just what Jesus taught. I broaden that reference to include all of what the Scriptures say. All of Scripture tells us what to expect when we spend eternity with the Lord, and it tells us how to get there. All of this can be called *The Good News*. Telling others is spreading *The Good News,* or *evangelization.*

    I completed my three years of study and formation to be certified as a Lay Ecclesial Minister in the year 2002 in Harrisburg, Pennsylvania. Later, at a gathering with my fellow classmates, I put a question to the group. I asked what the

"New Evangelization" asked us to do in our lives. These are some of the responses plus my reflections to the answers.

Ed said that we need to break from old methods. We need to be pro-active so as to be open to allowing the Holy Spirit to empower us. We should place our trust totally into the hands of the Spirit and allow the Spirit to totally guide us. This is obviously something we have not been accustomed to doing. We like to be "in charge" and be the creative ones. But when I am asked to lead people in a prayer, I've noticed that if I allow the Spirit to totally take over, that it is not I who am praying but the impetus of the Spirit that is doing the praying. Yes, it is through me but it is not truly "me."

Terry then suggested that we need to go back to serving the basic needs of people. We need to start with the methods used by Jesus, by serving the sick and the poor and always showing love and acceptance. We shouldn't be formal, academic, or distant but just be human to those humans in need.

Jim said that instead of always seeking holiness in "groups," we should stress development of our personal and individual holiness. Then we need to inspire others through being a strong witness for the Lord.

Linda reminded us that the Sacrament of Baptism calls us to holiness, each and every one. But these times are different from the past and are vastly in motion and changing. Hence, we are more challenged to know our faith very well, and not just to know it but to speak our faith. We have more "fallen-away" and "cafeteria" Catholics now, so we need to express our faith boldly and with love.

Christine added that what appear as stumbling blocks to us can be great opportunities in disguise. We must always look for and seek the "giftedness" in others.

Ed added that we must first seek God (seek the kingdom first), and all else will follow. We cannot ever become "self-satisfied," but must take up our cross daily and give ourselves daily to Jesus.

Doris also reminded us that the Lord works with people where they are, and not where we would like them to be. Hence, so must we.

Terry said that there is a strong pull, or current, in society which works against faith and that most people often live by and act on the current values in society, whatever they are.

Nella added that as highly trained Catholics, our priests need to know us well and use our training and our gifts.

Mark indicated that he is highly involved with the public, in general, and that about eighty percent of those he deals with are not "into" religion or faith. Hence, we need to first provide the basic sustenance by a strong witness in our living. We *must* project the *joy* of our faith in our lives. Why? Because we can catch more souls with honey than with vinegar.

Jim again affirmed that our seeking holiness is *essential*.

Illiterate Nation

Why is the United States so illiterate? Why are people not reading books—especially the classics, good novels, philosophy books, etc.?

I might be dating myself (though at my age that doesn't matter), but during the days of existentialism in Europe, the dock workers labored hard in the day, and at night visited the local bars to have some beers and debate the merits of those theories, especially those of Jean Paul Sartre. These were mostly uneducated people, but they read and discussed.

Does that ever happen here in this country, except in some colleges? Even in college, the only time I heard that type of discussion taking place was among those fellow students studying Latin and Greek and reading the Classics. Other well-educated and well-read people, just didn't discuss such areas of studies. Maybe they studied these books but barely ever discussed them.

Why didn't they? What is wrong with being willing to discuss ideas? Why do people only talk about what will make you money, or what you might want to own, or where you want to travel to, or what status symbol car you want to drive?

Why not read the classics, or important novels, or science fiction that deal with ideas of what the world and the universe is like, or the purpose of society? There are so many points to discuss but such talks just don't take place. Should they? If we wish to grow in understanding and thinking abilities, I suggest that the answer is yes.

What would these discussion do? They would help us want to learn more and sharpen our ideas. Once people see that they are growing in knowledge and honing and sharpening and developing their theories and their understanding, they will grow in self-respect and justified and deserving pride.

We are never too old to learn. If we stop learning or developing, we diminish our desire to live well. We might want to continue to exist but for humans, that is not enough.

Even for many types of animals, simply to exist is not enough. If you observe their actions in herds you notice how they care for others which might be in need, the needs that only others in the herd can give. They seek to protect the less able so that they can continue to live and develop in the community of the herd.

Simply existing doesn't help us, unless we are recuperating from a very serious illness or surgery. Otherwise we need physical stimulation such as food and exercise, but more importantly we need both intellectual and spiritual development and stimulation. We grow in mind and soul by such stimuli. Otherwise we simply vegetate and exist without growth or developments. Millions are living this type of existence, and this is a tremendous loss of our humanity, in my opinion.

Nation Without a Place for Mary

Naturally, I am speaking about Mary, the mother of Jesus. In Mexico in the sixteenth century, there lived a poor and uneducated peasant named Juan Diego. The Blessed Mother Mary appeared to him and asked him to give a message to the local bishop. Mary wanted Juan Diego to tell the bishop that she would like to have a church built there at that spot on Tepeyac Hill. Some interactions continued between Mary and the bishop, through Juan. Finally the bishop asked for a convincing sign from Mary, in order for him to believe that this was an actual, valid message from Heaven. The sign came and a church was established, and believers have flocked there to praise God and to pray.

Thus Mexico has a site where Mary appeared, and many faith-filled people go there to pray to her Son in gratitude and humility.

Do the people pray to Mary? Basically they pray to her Son. If they do address their prayers to Mary, it is to thank her or to ask her to take their requests to her Son, Jesus.

A somewhat similar occurrence took place in Portugal near the village of Fatima. Three young children who were, like Juan, poor, very uneducated, but, like Juan, devout and prayerful, saw the Blessed Virgin Mary. She made certain requests of them. When asked for a sign, she performed the Miracle of the Sun. It was the day that seventy thousand persons witnessed and watched, in shock, as the sun appeared to spin in the sky and hurtle towards the earth.

Such was the sign, and a church was built. Many, many, many people, from all over the world, travel to Fatima to pray and to praise the Lord. In fact, like Guadalupe, people come by the millions every year.

And thus Portugal has a site where Mary has appeared and many faith-filled people go there. They pray to her Son, or they ask Mary to take their requests directly to her Son and they thank her for how she helps.

Have you seen paintings of Mary holding her infant Son? Look at those pictures as they were drawn or painted down through the centuries. Look at Mary's arms. She is often depicted as holding her infant Son in one arm and the other arm leads to and points directly at her Son. Mary always directs us towards her Son and invites the world to come to, and be with, her Son.

In a village in France, Mary again appeared in the small village of Lourdes, to an uneducated, young peasant girl named Bernadette. Mary appeared many times to Bernadette, and she asked her to tell the local priest that she, Mary, wished to have a church built at that location. Again the message was given, and, again, the priest was highly skeptical. He wanted to know the Lady's name and he wanted a sign. It was given. Mary told Bernadette to dig in the dirt and to drink the water she found. She scraped the ground, and it seemed that little or no water came out. The people laughed and sneered at Bernadette. But as they were leaving, water began to flow. Now millions flock there to bathe in the water while asking for cures. The water has been tested many times and the results show plain water each time, and yet many receive cures.

The church was built. In fact there are three churches there now. Thus France has a site where Mary appeared and many faith-filled people go there to pray.

North America does not have a Marian shrine like Mexico, France, and Portugal. Why not? We do not know. Are we faithless in our love of the Lord? Do we not have love and devotion towards

God? Possibly we do not. We are a materialistic nation and that might be a hindrance for us.

Even so, we can implore the Lord to establish such a location here in this country. Or maybe we ought to ask for several locations for Mary to appear and ask for a church to be established.

My wife and I were members of a pilgrimage to such shrines. We were amazed to see the amount of people coming to pray and give praise to the Lord. Even if no physical miracle took place, the most significant, observable miracle was the movement of the hearts of all towards the Lord. They experienced a *conversion*. The primary meaning of this word does not mean a person's changing from one faith system to another. Rather it means a movement of one's heart, turning more and more to God.

Such mass conversions would highly increase the love of the Lord in huge numbers of persons. And since God is Love, the increase of love for Him in the hearts of Americans would bring a shining surge of holiness in our great nation.

 **About Leonine Publishers**

Leonine Publishers LLC makes fine Catholic literature available to Catholics throughout the English-speaking world. Leonine Publishers offers an innovative "hybrid" approach to book publication that helps authors as well as readers. Please visit our web site at www.leoninepublishers.com to learn more about us. Browse our online bookstore to find more solid Catholic titles to uplift, challenge, and inspire.

Our patron and namesake is Pope Leo XIII, a prudent, yet uncompromising pope during the stormy years at the close of the 19th century. Please join us as we ask his intercession for our family of readers and authors.

Do you have a book inside you? Visit our web site today. Leonine Publishers accepts manuscripts from Catholic authors like you. If your book is selected for publication, you will have an active part in the production process. This book is an example of our growing selection of literature for the busy Catholic reader of the 21st century.

www.leoninepublishers.com

www.ingramcontent.com/pod-product-compliance
Lightning Source LLC
Chambersburg PA
CBHW061329040426
42444CB00011B/2841